Tools for Practicing God's Presence in Everyday Life

presenceuniversity.com

If found, please let me know:

The Five Minute Jesus Journal

Ignite Your Life with God's Presence
Through Whole-Brain Gratitude

presenceuniversity.com

Presence University

CONNECT WITH US:
presenceuniversity.com
info@presenceu.com

CREATED BY
Brent McIntosh

EDITED BY
Pat Novak & Timbrel Veen

Published by Presence University

All Scripture quotations, unless otherwise indicated, are taken from the Holy Bible, New International Version®, NIV®. Copyright ©1973, 1978, 1984, 2011 by Biblica, Inc.™ Used by permission of Zondervan. All rights reserved worldwide. www.zondervan.com The "NIV" and "New International Version" are trademarks registered in the United States Patent and Trademark Office by Biblica, Inc.

©2021 Presence University. All Rights reserved. All material in this book may not be reproduced, transmitted, or distributed in any form without the written permission of Presence University.

To God seekers who go the distance.
You're the light in this world.

Ask and it will be given to you;
seek and you will find;
knock and the door will be opened to you.
For everyone who asks receives;
the one who seeks finds
and to the one who knocks,
the door will be opened.

Jesus
Matthew 7:7-8 NIV

You've already opened the door.

Now step in...

Jesus is the greatest treasure

In this life

And in the life to come.

Like any great relationship,

It starts with taking the time.

How to Use This Journal

Have fun with it.

Seriously. Enjoy the journey.

Whatever your future holds, it's on God's heart

for you to encounter more presence,

to experience more love.

Contents

Five Ways We believe God Wants to Use This Journal to Transform *YOUR LIFE*... 1

The Five Main Actions.. 3

Start with THANKS.. 5

Title & Describe Your Specific Positive Memory................ 9

Five Sense Words.. 15

Be Present in Your Memory.. 17

Feeling Words... 21

Stick-Sketch It!... 23

Look for Jesus or Where You Sense the Most Joy or Peace.... 27

40 Day Dare.. 33

The Journal... 35

Five Ways We Believe God Wants to Use This Journal to Transform *YOUR LIFE* are to:

- *GROW* your connection with Jesus and your awareness of his presence.

- *MAKE* you more resilient to life's challenges.

- *BUILD* more joy in your life.

- *IGNITE* connections with your family and friends.

- Help you *SUSTAIN* a lifestyle of encountering Jesus with you.

Why?

- It's do-able, even if you don't journal.

- It helps to remember the good things God does.

- It helps puzzle-piece together an album of good stories in your heart and with others.

- It will show you how just a few minutes daily can harness your experiences as altar moments to access God's presence.

- It's one of the easiest ways to build greater connections in your brain.

- It helps people heal.

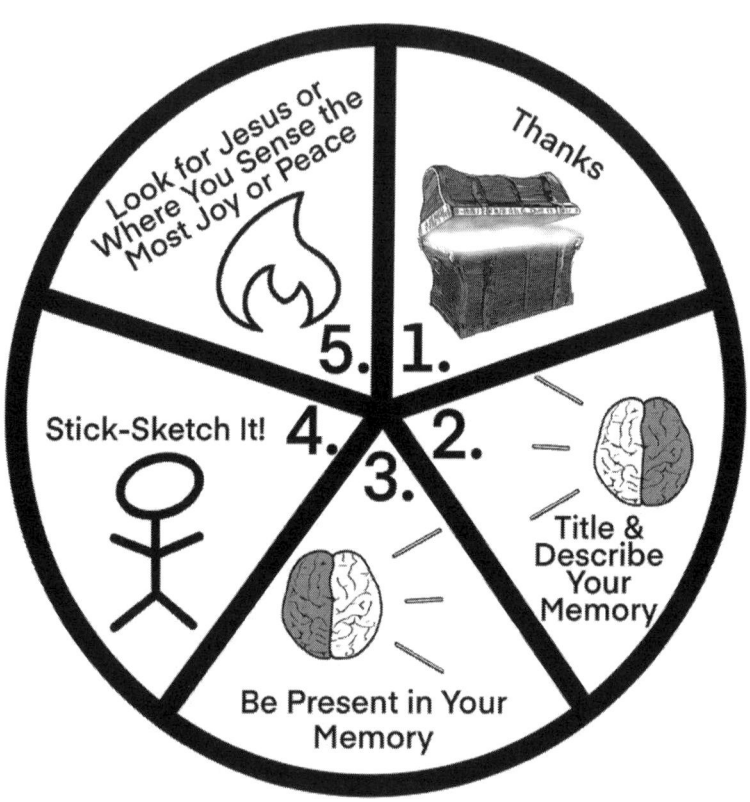

The Five Main Actions

Thanks
I am thankful for…

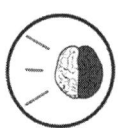
Title and Describe Your Memory
Jesus, what specific positive memory would be good for me to focus on in this moment? (30-60 seconds nothing comes to mind? Pick a memory & continue.)

Be Present in Your Memory
Take a moment. Allow yourself to experience the memory. Close your eyes and picture being present in this specific memory. Use your 5 senses. (Smell the outdoors, feel the liquid of the ocean envelope you, etc.) What did this memory feel like?

Stick Sketch It!
Sketch a stick-figure-picture of this memory on the page to the left.

Look for Jesus OR Where You Sense the Most Joy or Peace
Ask, "Jesus, would you show me where you were in this memory?" If you sense his presence or see where he was, draw something to show where (cross, flame, etc.) OR draw where you sensed the most joy or peace

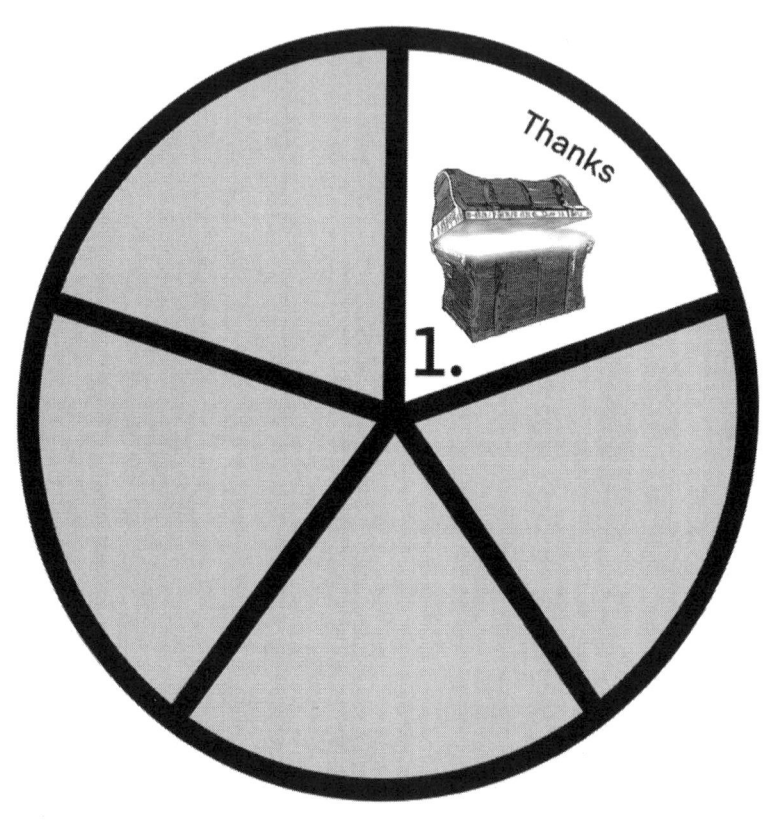

Start with THANKS

I am thankful for…

Start with THANKS! Thankfulness is one of the easiest ways to start transforming your life *right now*. It increases joy, and research shows it improves our well-being. The Bible tells us something similar.

For starters, the Bible talks about how to start with God, how to approach him. Psalm 100:4 says, "Enter his gates with thanksgiving and his courts with praise; give thanks to him and praise his name." This is a great verse. It's foundational in how to draw near to God. It says to *enter*, to *start*, with thanksgiving.

The Passion Translation words the same verse like this, "You can pass through his open gates with the password of praise. Come right into his presence with thanksgiving. Come bring your thank offering to him and affectionately bless his beautiful name!" I love that! The verse literally shows a secret to the kingdom of heaven, a secret on how to connect with God. Thankfulness is our first step into God's presence. Praise and *thanksgiving* are the password. What do you like about God? What are you thankful for? This is the way to begin connecting in a deep relationship with God, an easy way to begin sustaining more of what God is doing in your life.

So, each journal moment starts with a short list of things you're thankful for. Look through recent moments for the treasures of the recent past. Look past the dirt of the day and toward your treasured moments. Build a treasure chest of thankfulness. Many years ago, there was a Calvin and Hobbes comic called "There's Treasure Everywhere." Calvin and Hobbes were right. Always be on the lookout.

Build a treasure chest of thankfulness.

This practice primes the pump, taps into the well of God inside you and gets things started so you can build a pattern that becomes easier to connect with God. You might start with simple stuff like your last meal, or the breath you're breathing right now. The first time I tried doing this I couldn't think of what I was thankful for. It was difficult for me. It took me awhile. I had been a pastor for many years at that point. I knew how to enter God's presence by pouring my heart and my emotions out to him, but I did not know how to enter his presence through thankfulness, and thankfulness is the easiest way.

This journal focuses on positive memories, specific moments and things you're thankful for. Why? Because this turns on your relational connectedness. It works in all of our relationships, not just our relationship with God. Like the picture below, thankfulness turns on the *friend settings* in our brains. It's like connecting up to a local Wi-Fi connection with your phone.

Thankfulness may be a brand-new practice for you, and like everything you practice, practice makes powerful. If thankfulness is hard for you, there's good news. It gets easier!

Through practicing thankfulness, you will begin finding more joy and security in your life. Practicing a lifestyle of thanks rewires your brain. Pictures of the brain show how this is possible, how the brain is moldable (often called neuroplasticity). Your brain can grow new pathways, an entire new network of pathways for healing, connectedness, or new skills. This is good news! If you've been stuck, or if you've struggled with a strong negative emotion (fear, depression, loneliness, etc.), there is real hope. Your brain pathways can change! You can change your mind patterns.

Authentic thankfulness is the first step to stepping out of being stuck in negative feelings. In other words, transformation is something you can practice with Jesus. God knew this a long time ago and encourages us this way, "Be transformed by the renewing of your mind" (Romans 12:2). Transformation is most effective if you practice it as a lifestyle, and that is why this journal was created.

Doing It Looks Something Like This:

 *I am thankful for...*

1. Our dog Rocket - made me feel safe today.

2. Dinner & playing cards with the family - Carne Asada tacos!!

3. My black jacket - the way Jesus helped me feel covered.

    Thankfulness might be as simple and short as one or two words each line, or it might be a little more detailed. The key is consistency. If you get off track, start back up again.

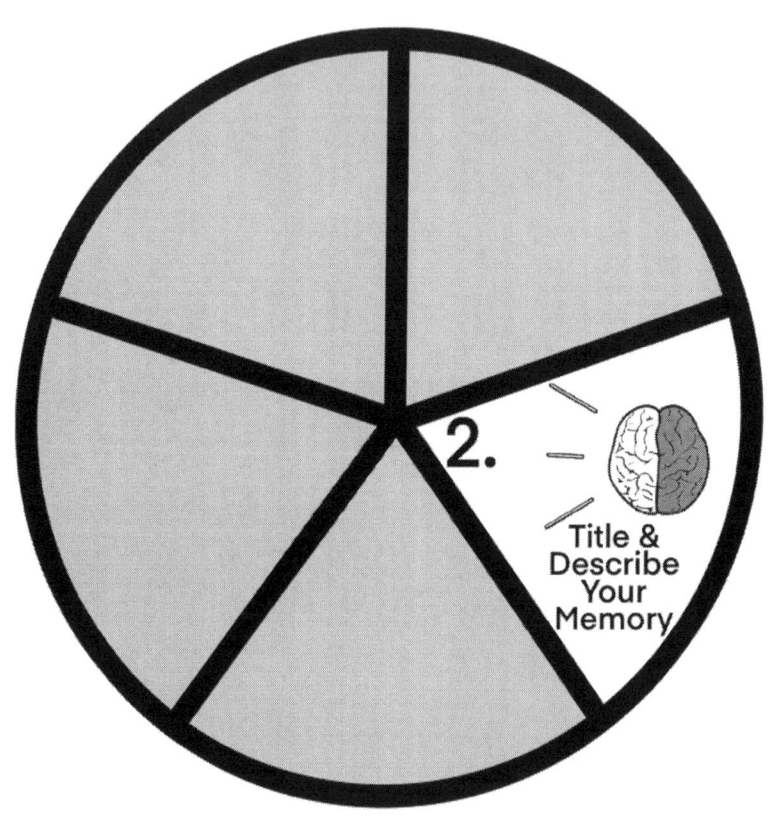

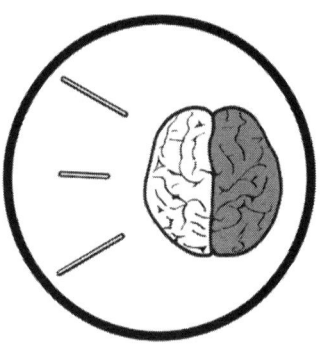

2. Title & Describe Your Specific Positive Memory

Jesus, what specific positive memory would be good for me to focus on in this moment? (30-60 seconds nothing comes to mind? Pick one & continue on.)

The power to title AND describe. Each app on a phone has an icon or some kind of picture and a word or two that name the app. Have you thought about that? This is working both sides of your brain. The picture speaks to the right side of your brain and the app title speaks to the language/left side of your brain (see pictures on the following page).

What if there weren't any pictures for your apps, only words? Every time a person went to use their phone they would have to scroll through a bunch of black and white words to find their apps and wouldn't be able to quickly tap on the app icon. Or what if the opposite were true? If there were only pictures and no way to search that one app by name that you can't remember? This would be confusing one way or the other, so we use both, engaging both sides of the brain. In this step, choose a specific positive memory. Describe some of the basic details. This practices remembering with both sides of your brain.

Neuroscience mini-course. Each year I taught high school Bible class, my students chose to use either a lined or unlined journal.

The start of each class was God time. They did things like drawing pictures of verses, writing them out, or writing God a letter, etc. It was one of their favorite times. Each year I was surprised how the number of students was split down the middle with half of the students choosing lines and half without. Which would you be?

Whichever you lean toward, challenge yourself. Live whole-brained. Don't be critical of the side different from your leaning. Otherwise, the smartest you can ever be is only half-brained.

Like every brain, yours is split into two hemispheres, two halves that work differently. One of the halves functions best on orderly measured lines while the other does best with the freedom of a blank page.

Your left brain is your language brain. It is logical, literal, linear, and labeling. Your right brain is your picture brain. It is creative, out of the box, emotional and sees in shapes or pictures. Sometimes they don't always agree.

For years now, technology has been able to take pictures of the brain while it's active, showing that the more your brain practices walking over the bridge between the two sides of the brain, the stronger, faster, and bigger that bridge becomes between the two. One of the ways to do this is through naming (the left/language brain) our emotions (the right/picture brain). Naming a memory and using a few words to describe it starts this connecting process, building your brain bridges. Why is this important? Well, not only does this exercise your brain's connectedness, creating wider highways for more information to travel, but it begins helping *both sides* of your brain to *remember*.

Remember with your whole brain.
Why is whole-brain gratitude important to remember? In Deuteronomy, God is constantly reminding the people of Israel to remember. "Remember the day you stood before the Lord," "Remember that you were slaves," "Remember well what the Lord your God did to Pharaoh," or "Remember how the Lord your God led you all the way in the wilderness these forty years." On and on God said, *remember*. But again and again the people of Israel forgot. They probably didn't forget on the left side of their brains. They remembered the facts of what happened, but in their picture/experiencing

memory, they definitely forgot. They could no longer see God creatively might do something outside the box again, and they no longer cared about being connected with God.

A person can memorize a factual list of information through their left brain. This is important if you're getting a driver's license and need to remember the laws, or taking some kind of test in school, or measuring ingredients for a recipe, or memorizing a Bible verse. Here the left brain is at work.

Telling the story of a specific positive experience uses language (left brain) to describe the experience (right brain), bridging your remembering between both sides of the brain. For example, one of my favorite activities is kayaking in Dana Point Harbor. I remember last week how the cool breeze in the sun made me feel alive. It wasn't too hot or cold. The waters weren't stirred up and crazy like the time before. This time I felt peace and a sense of adventure. I felt God with me and like everything in my world was going to be ok. My dad recently passed, but here I felt God's presence with me. I was not alone. Describing through the five senses and feeling words helps bridge the left and right brain.

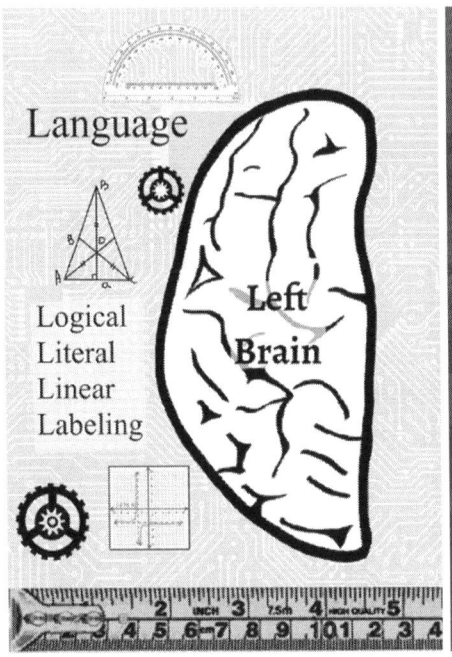
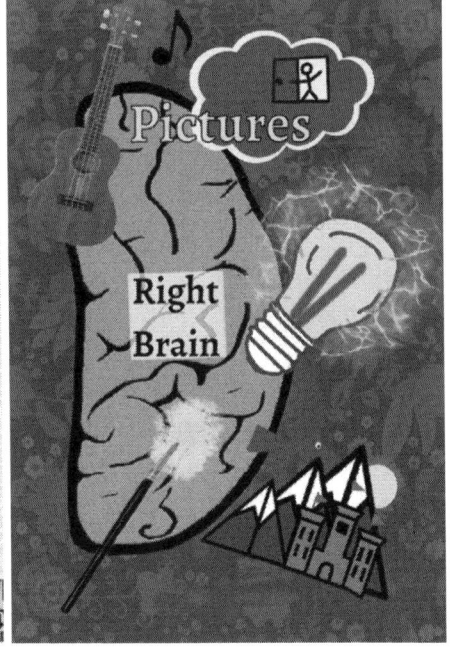

Notes on the five senses. If you need help describing some of the details of your memory, taking a moment to think about the five senses can be a help. With the best of your ability, be aware of the senses you experienced in your memory. What did you smell, taste, hear, see, or physically feel? It's ok if you didn't sense all five. Maybe you only experienced a couple of them. Write key words for the ones you encountered. *There's a five-sense word list at the end of this chapter to help you.

Practice whole-brain remembering. Stories are one of the easiest ways to be whole-brained. Stories of thankfulness are one of the easiest ways to build healthy connections in your own life, in connection with others, and in connection with God. Practicing thankful remembering is important on both sides of the brain. Otherwise, we aren't allowing the goodness of positive experiences to fully affect us.

Try this. Make an ok symbol with one hand (thumb and pointer finger pressed together) and make a peace sign with your other hand (pointer finger and middle finger up). *Switch* (do the ok symbol and peace symbol with opposite hands). *Switch again.* Back and forth trade off as quickly as you can. This is a simple form of crossing one of the bridges where the left and right sides of your brain bridge together. The left side of your brain operates the right side of your body and the right side of your brain, the left side of your body. Bridging the left and right brain helps integrate memories from the two sides. Bridging through remembering positive moments with whole-brain gratitude brings healing and makes us more resilient.

Why "Positive"?
Aim for a positivity ratio of at least 3 to 1. This means that for every heart wrenching negative emotional experience you endure, you experience at least three heartfelt positive emotional experiences that uplift you.
Barbara Fredrickson
Positivity

Or as Philippians 4:8 says, "Finally, brothers and sisters, whatever is true, whatever is noble, whatever is right, whatever is pure, whatever is lovely, whatever is admirable—if anything is excellent or praiseworthy—think about such things." This isn't just about being positive. It's about practicing heaven mindedness in ways the Bible shows us. Just like a movie has music playing in the background, you have emotional memory playing in the background of your life like an emotional soundtrack.

Life is like a Bluetooth speaker you can hook up to different connections - soundtracks with different emotional experiences playing in the background. We go through terrible things sometimes, but God is always doing something, even in the midst of our greatest pains. Practicing a life connected to a soundtrack of real thankfulness opens up new roads, unseen doors that wouldn't be there without gratitude. So, take these moments, no matter what's going on in your life, to practice remembering thankfulness with your whole brain. This is a practice in putting our ears up to the goodness God's put in our path and then amplifying it.

Ask Jesus. When you are looking for a specific positive memory to name and describe, pause briefly and ask Jesus what specific positive memory is good for you to focus on in this moment. Wait. Listen. If you don't sense Jesus highlighting anything, no worries. This is just practice - practice hearing. After 30-60 seconds, go ahead and pick a specific positive memory so you don't get stuck on this step and are able to enter deeper into thankfulness and connection. It might be something simple. It might be only a few sentences like my kayak story.

Doing It Looks Something Like This:

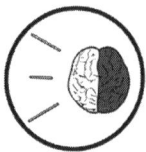 *Jesus, what specific positive memory would be good for me to focus on in this moment? (30-60 seconds nothing comes to mind? Pick a memory & continue)*

Kayaking in the harbor.

Some details in this memory are…

The cool breeze and the warmth of the sun made me feel alive.

It wasn't too hot or cold.

The waters were calm, not stirred up and crazy like last time.

*Use the five sense words on the next page to help you.

Five Sense Words
Some Five Sense words I experienced in this specific positive memory are:

taste
sweet, sour, bitter, bland, cool, chewy, crunchy, salty, savory, dry, fizzy, juicy, hot, cold, creamy, sugary, acidic, tangy, tasteless

touch
cold, hot, wet, warm, dry, cool, prickly, rough, fuzzy, hard, soft, silky, smooth, sticky, heavy, thick, light, bumpy, spiky, sharp, gooey, icy, lukewarm, wooden, cuddly, chilly, damp, breezy, dusty, fluffy, rocky, slimy, slippery, tight

sight
shiny, long, skinny, fat, thin, small, large, colorful, speckled, light, dark, bright, dotted, clean, dirty, woodsy, flat, flickering, freckled, huge

smell
fresh, salty, smoky, sour, spicy, sweet, stinky, clean, earthy, new, old, minty, musty, mellow, flowery

hear
loud, noisy, quiet, silent, creaky, squeaky, gurgling, crunching, laughing, thud, thump, whisper, bang, buzz, melodic, fizzy, faint

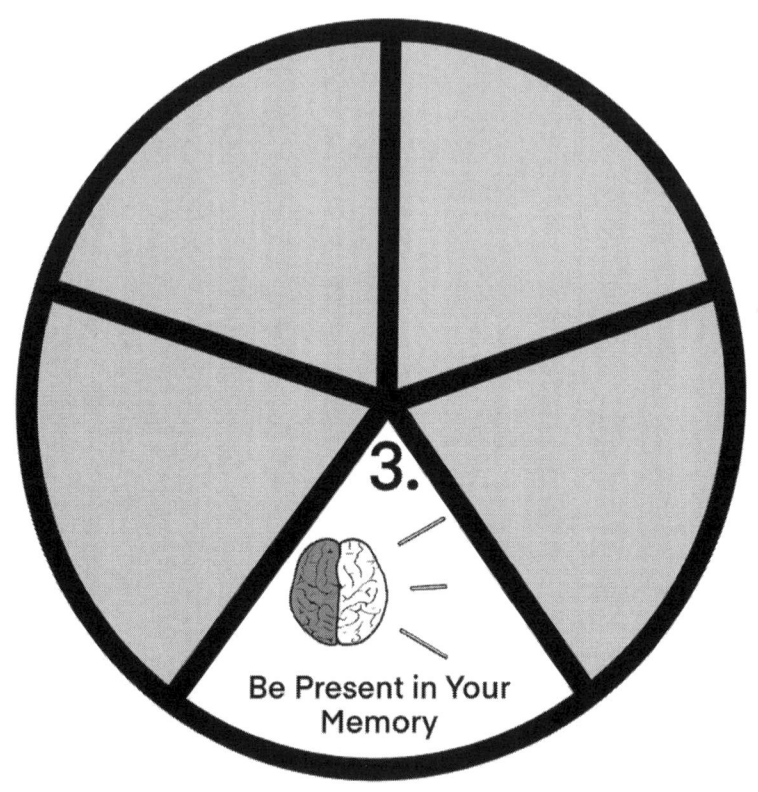

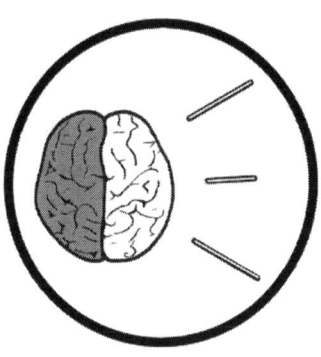

3. Be Present in Your Memory

Take a moment. Allow yourself to experience the memory. Close your eyes and picture being present in this specific memory. See with your 5 senses. (Smell the outdoors, feel the liquid of the ocean envelope you, etc.) What did this memory feel like?

Can you "see" a memory with your eyes closed? If I asked you to close your eyes and said the word "dog," can you picture a dog? What kind of dog do you picture? Close your eyes and try for a moment. If you own a dog, you probably pictured your dog. Whatever picture you had of a dog would probably be a different picture than someone else's "dog," with different memories, positive or negative, connected to that "dog." Or if I asked you to remember the time you ate your favorite meal, would you be able to see yourself eating it? Can you think about a favorite memory? Or a favorite person and what it was like being with them when your eyes are closed? For some people this ability is difficult. If that's you, don't worry about it. Sometimes it just takes practice.

Start by closing your eyes and thinking of one of your favorite foods to eat. Or think of someone you know (a brother, sister, or friend). You might first think of their face, or a memory of an experience with them. If the person is someone close to you it's rare to think of their name first without a picture of their face, or a memory, or feeling you have when you're with them. People rarely think about a person's name first when it is someone close to them. They might say the name, but without realizing it we often focus on the emotional imagery that comes to mind when thinking of that person. This is because our brains access the picture/experiential (right brain) a little faster than language (left brain).

We live in a fast food, instant-streaming, I-want-it-right-now culture. We rarely take the time to fully absorb what's happening in the moment. We are often too busy swiping past, looking for the next thing.

With the best of your ability, don't look at your specific memory from the outside looking in. Instead, step into it. Be in the memory, looking through your eyes in the memory. Allow yourself to experience any of the five senses you wrote down in the previous section.

Eyes of the heart. This isn't about making things up that weren't a part of the memory. Instead, we are practicing remembering what actually happened, with the experiential, right side of our picture/movie brain.

For example. One of my favorite memories about my dad is a time we were at a park down the street from my house. I had been an adult for a long time already and had kids of my own. We were flying kites. My dad was not a man of many words, but that day he was full of God-hearted wisdom speaking to me about not worrying about troubles I was having at my job, but trusting in God. I remember the breeze, how it was cool outside, but sunny. It was a beautiful day. The Lord was with us so strong that day. I felt God's presence in my dad, felt God's peace. I felt secure, like everything really would be ok.

What did this memory feel like? Above I gave some examples. Naming what we feel is incredibly powerful. In the past few years, naming our emotions have been identified as one of the most powerful ways to practice relational vulnerability and connection. Throughout Christian therapy models as well as psychology texts I had in my PsyD program; healthy families *name* their feelings. We practice the same in our relationship with Jesus.

David was great at naming emotions. From negative feelings in Psalm 69:19-20 "I am scorned, disgraced, and shamed...scorn has broken my heart," to Psalm 16:11 where he says, "In Your presence is fullness of joy, in your right hand are pleasures evermore."

Doing It Looks Something Like This:

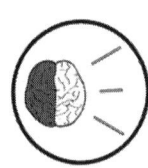 *Take a moment. Allow yourself to experience the memory. Close your eyes and picture being present in this specific memory. Use your five senses. (Smell the outdoors, feel the liquid of the ocean envelope you, etc.)*

What did this memory feel like?

I felt peace and a sense of adventure.

*Use the feeling words on the next page to help you. Choose 1-3 of them.

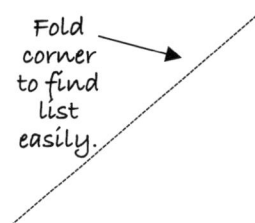
Fold corner to find list easily.

Feeling Words
In this specific positive memory, I feel...

happy
glad, satisfied, thrilled, encouraged, gratified, joyful, overjoyed, relieved, fortunate

amazed
stunned, fascinated, surprised, awe, speechless, enlightened, wonderment

secure
curious, open, eager, optimistic, bold, generous, accepting, kind, receptive, understanding, confident, free, satisfied, thankful, grateful, positive, self-assured, confident, interested

compassionate
loving, refreshed, affectionate, cozy, passionate, warm, tender, responsive, appreciative, comforted, vulnerable

excited
alive, playful, energetic, resourced, enthusiastic, rejuvenated, talkative, motivated, fun-filled, driven, determined, jittery, renewed

peaceful
relieved, at ease, relaxed, calm, comforted, cool, protected, composed, quieted, rested

4. Stick-Sketch It!

Sketch a stick-figure picture of this memory.

It's not about art. Have you ever asked a child to draw a picture? If they're young enough, they'll usually jump at the chance. They'll draw whatever you ask. But then, somewhere between kindergarten and 5th grade they often start responses like, "Oh, I can't draw," or "I'm not that good."

Whatever the reason, Jesus doesn't want you to live in less than he's made you to be. Jesus is about freedom. Maybe you experienced the negativity of someone else, but those are core places Jesus wants to pour his love into.

We all experience negative emotions at one time or another, but what if you could tap into the childlike part of your heart and discover childlike healing and childlike memory? Jesus said it this way, "...Unless you change and become like little children, you will never enter the kingdom of heaven," (Matthew 19:3). Whaaat?!? That is one of the most powerful verses in the Bible, so often overlooked. We don't enter unless we become like children. God's invitation is, change, be more childlike.

The disciples asked, "Who is the greatest in the kingdom of heaven?" Jesus says we enter from the low place. He says, "Therefore, whoever takes the lowly position of this *child* is the greatest in the kingdom of heaven. And whoever welcomes one such child in my name welcomes me," (Matthew 18:4-5). "We have to allow ourselves to be tender, even toward our own weaknesses. Give yourself permission to sketch, to be childlike again.

This section doesn't have to do with artistic ability. It is about recording your memory with the right side of your brain, creating an icon for your memory. This increases memory retrieval and access on the right side of the brain.

Why stick figures? Again, sketching stick figure pictures is not about art. You are not trying to create an art piece here. Maybe somewhere down the line artwork will come out of it, but that's not the goal here. For example, think about the following symbol:

It can symbolize a few things but is universally known as the symbol for eternity. The infinity symbol never ends. It is eternal. Everyone knows this. BUT it is nothing even close to what eternity really is. It is a symbol for eternity.

We use symbols all the time because they simplify and help us communicate in quick terms (similar to the earlier example of the app icons).

Stick sketching your experiences is like that. You're creating a playlist of experiences more readily accessible to the picture side of your brain. A stick sketch is stored in a different section of your brain. Sketching a memory can cause greater recall and help you better remember the experience through your five senses and emotions.

Pictures and words. Think about the first words. They were pictures, hieroglyphics painted on cavern walls. The first words were pictographs, words with pictures in them. They were a combination of word and image, a remembering on both sides of the brain. In a way, this process is like drawing the hieroglyphics of your gratitude. If you'd like to see examples of Hebrew picture letters, see www.jewishrootsstudy.org.

Again and again Jesus spoke to the picture side of the brain through things such as, "The kingdom of heaven is like..." and would then talk about farming or family or other word pictures that would communicate an emotional

24

imagery imprint on the picture side of the brain. Recording our thankfulness through simple sketches helps us remember details and experiences more fully so we don't just remember the facts of what happened, but we remember the experience like an altar of experience we can revisit.

Doing It Looks Something Like This:

Sketch a stick-figure-picture of this memory on the page to the left. (Include a stick sketch with the details you wrote earlier).

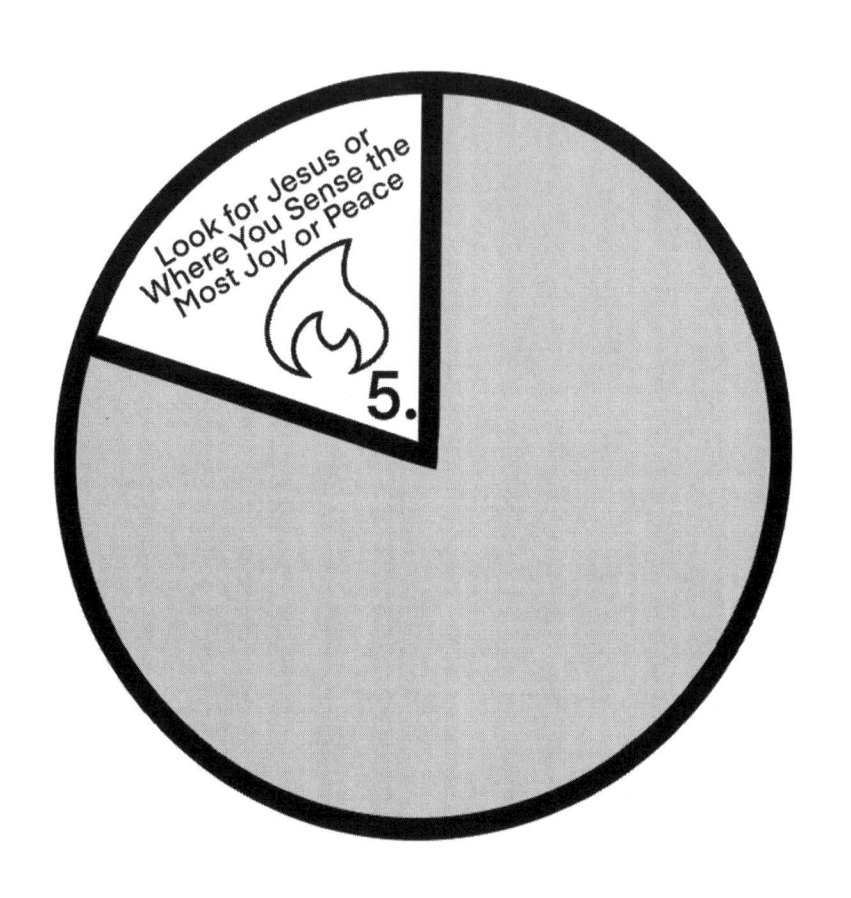

5. Look for Jesus or Where You Sense the Most Joy or Peace

5. Look for Jesus OR Where You Sense the Most Joy or Peace

Ask, "Jesus, would you show me where you were in this memory?" If you sense his presence or see where he was, draw something to show where (cross, flame, stick figure Jesus, etc.) **OR** *Draw where you sensed the most joy or peace.*

Practice God's presence. Practicing your awareness of God's presence is the greatest thing a person can practice. According to what we looked at earlier, your brain creates networks around thankfulness and praise, accessing God's network through the secret password. What if you wanted to get on a wi-fi network but didn't have the password? God is giving you *His*. (Psalm 100:4-5 TPT)

In studying the brain, Donald Hebb made a startling discovery in the brain more than 70 years ago...

Neurons that fire together, wire together.

This is a crazy statement. This is why thankfulness is so powerful! What your brain gets excited about wires greater pathways of attachment and connection, building bigger highways, widening your brain's bandwidth and transferring more data (whether feelings, thoughts or Holy Spirit). The Bible says it this way, "Delight yourself in the Lord, and he will give you the desires of your heart" (Psalm 37:4 ESV). God's 1 Samuel highway is for you to access (Isaiah 35:8), but you've got to use the password (thankfulness), and take time on God's network, enjoying what's on your path.

Remember, God doesn't hide things from you. He hides things *for* you. Like a loving parent with an easter egg hunt set up in the front yard for their kids, if the parent drove over a few streets and put eggs in a park, it wouldn't make any sense. The kid would never find them. God hides things *for* you to find. What does heaven look like for you today? Heaven is the God-human Jesus, and God has more for you.

If you get stuck? Sometimes it might be easy to sense Jesus' presence in your memory. Sometimes it might not. If not, that's ok. If negative or bad feelings come up, push past them. Sometimes we try to force it. If so, return to thankfulness. Be kind to yourself. Kindness is still a fruit of the spirit (Galatians 5:22). If you're straining, working really hard to hear God, sometimes you can shut off the *friend settings* in your brain (like we talked about earlier) and no longer be relational, like putting relational connectedness in airplane mode. We often do this with God, treating him like something other than he is, maybe like a vending machine for our needs. But God is relational.

Jesus said, "So it is with your prayers. Ask and you'll receive. Seek and you'll discover. Knock on heaven's door, and it will one day open for you. Every persistent person will receive what he asks for. Every persistent seeker will discover what he needs. And everyone who knocks persistently will one day find an open door," (Luke 11:9-10 TPT). Seek and you will find. God will meet you.

If you only see a part of Jesus or sense his presence... If you don't see where Jesus is in your memory, there are lots of ways to persevere. Maybe you sense Jesus' presence behind you in the memory or maybe you see a part of him, like his feet. If so, lean in and ask Jesus, "Jesus, would you show me your face?" Wait. Be "in your memory," with your eyes closed and the eyes of your heart open.

If you don't see Jesus at all... Maybe practice looking for another person of the trinity. If you don't see Jesus, practice looking for Father God or Holy Spirit. In memories, sometimes we're more closed off to one of the persons in the trinity and just need to approach God through a different person in the trinity.

If you're still stuck... Be present "in" your memory, looking through the eyes of where you were in your memory. Be aware of where you sense the most joy or peace and sketch a symbol over that area (maybe a happy face or a peace symbol). The goal is to connect with God's presence, to connect with Jesus. If all you're sensing is the joy or peace of the memory though, lean in. That's awesome. Don't despise the moments of small beginnings of what Jesus might be building in you (Zechariah 4:10). It's just practice. Have fun. Enjoy God.

Important! This is not about creating your own imaginations of God. If anyone ever tells you to just "make it up," don't waste your time. Those are just fantasies. That can be dangerous. That can cause a person to begin following something that is not Jesus and might even be a kind of fake Jesus. To avoid this, don't make something up in the memory that's not there. Instead, practice your sensitivity to God's presence, practice sensing what God is actively doing. Look for Jesus. Remember Revelation 1? It is about the "unveiling" of Jesus. Sometimes we only see the veil. This journey is about looking past the veil, because Jesus made way for us to connect. Jesus tore the veil (Matthew 27:51).

It's like a story I heard about a recent addict giving his life to Jesus. Suddenly he understood God saying, "Oh, ok, it's like a drawbridge where God's half of the bridge is already down, ready to connect with us and it's up to us to bring our half down and connect with him." Yes, that's what it's like. This is an invitation to more. Take the time. Allow yourself to connect with God's presence.

*Take it a step further. After practicing a few journal moments with Jesus in the blank pages coming up, you might try taking it a step further. One way you can do this is by being aware of how Jesus' presence was specifically highlighted to you. Was there a particular *way* Jesus showed up to you? (For example, was Jesus compassionate, secure, bold, or playful?) If so, write it on the bottom line. If not, no worries.

Sometimes leaning in asking Jesus will show you more and other times just being with him is more than enough. Either way, take a moment and tell Jesus what you like about him or this memory.

Doing It Looks Something Like This:

Ask, "Jesus, would you show me where you were in this memory?" If you sense his presence or see where he was, draw something to show where (cross, flame, etc.) **OR** draw where you sensed the most joy or peace.

*Take a moment and thank Jesus for this memory and/or what you like about him.

Thank you, Jesus. I like how you make me feel secure & bold, how you remind me who I am & that you love me and you're always with me.

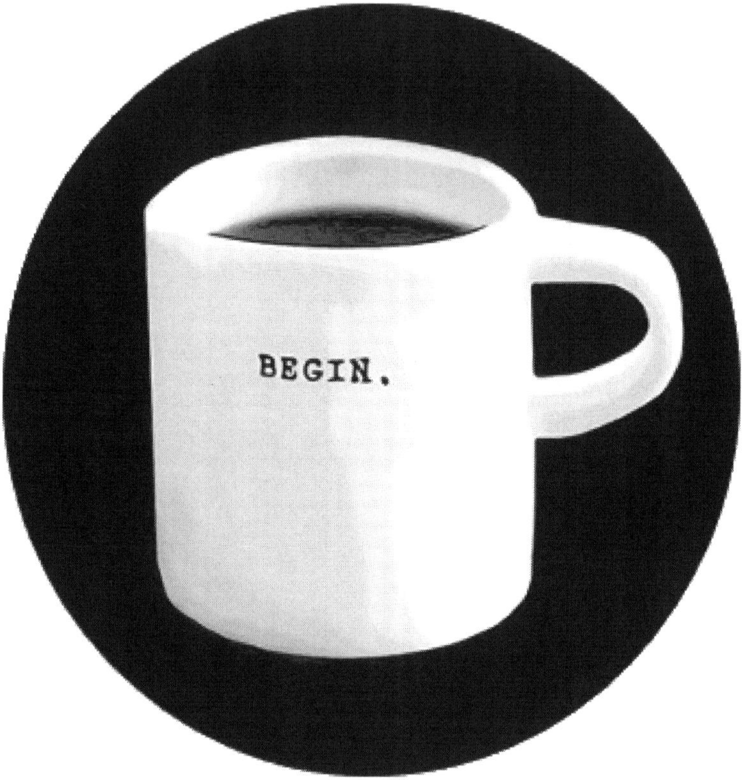
BEGIN.

40 Day Dare

There are 40 blank journal pages here.

This is your dare...

Do 40.

Maybe do 1 every day. Maybe more.
Maybe 5 each week.

The dare: Commit to completing 40 of them.

Experience what it does. Set yourself up to succeed. Pray. Commit to how many you're going to do. Check the box and fill in the blanks if you're in.

☐ I commit to do *The Five Minute Jesus Journal* – 40 Day Dare, to complete _____ (#of entries) each day/week (circle one) until I complete all 40.

Congratulations! A great way to be active in your transformation process with God is through commitment. It will encourage consistency, and that's the way you'll get the most out of this journal

/ /20

Rejoice always, pray continually, give thanks in all circumstances; for this is God's will for you in Christ Jesus. 1 Thessalonians 5:16-18

I am thankful for...
1. _____
2. _____
3. _____

Jesus, what specific positive memory would be good for me to focus on in this moment? (30-60 seconds nothing comes to mind? Pick a memory & continue.)

_____

Some details in this memory are... (Include 1-2 Five Sense words.)

_____

_____

_____

Take a moment. Allow yourself to experience the memory. Close your eyes. Picture being present in this specific memory. (Smell the trees, feel the liquid ocean envelope you, etc.) What did this memory feel like? (Include 1-3 Feeling Words.)

_____

Sketch a stick-figure-picture of this memory on the page to the left. (Include a stick sketch with the details you wrote above).

*Ask, "Jesus, would you show me where you were in this memory?" If you sense his presence or see where he was, draw something to show where (cross, flame, etc.) OR draw where you sensed the most joy or peace. *Take a moment and thank Jesus for this memory and/or what you like about Jesus.*

_____

_____

/   /20

Enter his gates with thanksgiving and his courts with praise; give thanks to him and praise his name. Psalm 100:4

I am thankful for...
1. _____
2. _____
3. _____

Jesus, what specific positive memory would be good for me to focus on in this moment? (30-60 seconds nothing comes to mind? Pick a memory & continue.)

_____

Some details in this memory are... (Include 1-2 Five Sense words.)

_____

_____

_____

Take a moment. Allow yourself to experience the memory. Close your eyes. Picture being present in this specific memory. (Smell the trees, feel the liquid ocean envelope you, etc.) What did this memory feel like? (Include 1-3 Feeling Words.)

_____

Sketch a stick-figure-picture of this memory on the page to the left. (Include a stick sketch with the details you wrote above).

Ask, "Jesus, would you show me where you were in this memory?" If you sense his presence or see where he was, draw something to show where (cross, flame, etc.) OR draw where you sensed the most joy or peace. *Take a moment and thank Jesus for this memory and/or what you like about Jesus.

_____

_____

/   /20

When all the Israelites saw the fire coming down and the glory of the Lord above the temple, they knelt on the pavement with their faces to the ground, and they worshiped and gave thanks to the Lord, saying, "He is good; his love endures forever." 2 Chronicles 7:3

I am thankful for...

1. _____

2. _____

3. _____

Jesus, what specific positive memory would be good for me to focus on in this moment? (30-60 seconds nothing comes to mind? Pick a memory & continue.)

_____

Some details in this memory are... (Include 1-2 Five Sense words.)

_____

_____

_____

Take a moment. Allow yourself to experience the memory. Close your eyes. Picture being present in this specific memory. (Smell the trees, feel the liquid ocean envelope you, etc.) What did this memory feel like? (Include 1-3 Feeling Words.)

_____

Sketch a stick-figure-picture of this memory on the page to the left. (Include a stick sketch with the details you wrote above).

*Ask, "Jesus, would you show me where you were in this memory?" If you sense his presence or see where he was, draw something to show where (cross, flame, etc.) OR draw where you sensed the most joy or peace. *Take a moment and thank Jesus for this memory and/or what you like about Jesus.*

_____

_____

/   /20

Taking the five loaves and the two fish and looking up to heaven, he gave thanks and broke the loaves. Matthew 14:19

I am thankful for...
1. _____
2. _____
3. _____

Jesus, what specific positive memory would be good for me to focus on in this moment? (30-60 seconds nothing comes to mind? Pick a memory & continue.)

_____

Some details in this memory are... (Include 1-2 Five Sense words.)

_____

_____

Take a moment. Allow yourself to experience the memory. Close your eyes. Picture being present in this specific memory. (Smell the trees, feel the liquid ocean envelope you, etc.) What did this memory feel like? (Include 1-3 Feeling Words.)

_____

Sketch a stick-figure-picture of this memory on the page to the left. (Include a stick sketch with the details you wrote above).

Ask, "Jesus, would you show me where you were in this memory?" If you sense his presence or see where he was, draw something to show where (cross, flame, etc.) OR draw where you sensed the most joy or peace. *Take a moment and thank Jesus for this memory and/or what you like about Jesus.

_____

_____

/ /20

No one can deny it—God is really good to Israel and to all those with pure hearts. But I nearly missed seeing it for myself. Psalm 73:1 TPT

I am thankful for...
1. _____

2. _____

3. _____

Jesus, what specific positive memory would be good for me to focus on in this moment? (30-60 seconds nothing comes to mind? Pick a memory & continue.)

_____

Some details in this memory are... (Include 1-2 Five Sense words.)

_____

_____

_____

Take a moment. Allow yourself to experience the memory. Close your eyes. Picture being present in this specific memory. (Smell the trees, feel the liquid ocean envelope you, etc.) What did this memory feel like? (Include 1-3 Feeling Words.)

_____

Sketch a stick-figure-picture of this memory on the page to the left. (Include a stick sketch with the details you wrote above).

*Ask, "Jesus, would you show me where you were in this memory?" If you sense his presence or see where he was, draw something to show where (cross, flame, etc.) OR draw where you sensed the most joy or peace. *Take a moment and thank Jesus for this memory and/or what you like about Jesus.*

_____

_____

/   /20

I will give thanks to you, Lord, with all my heart; I will tell of all your wonderful deeds. Psalm 9:1

I am thankful for...

1. _____

2. _____

3. _____

Jesus, what specific positive memory would be good for me to focus on in this moment? (30-60 seconds nothing comes to mind? Pick a memory & continue.)

_____

Some details in this memory are... (Include 1-2 Five Sense words.)

_____

_____

_____

Take a moment. Allow yourself to experience the memory. Close your eyes. Picture being present in this specific memory. (Smell the trees, feel the liquid ocean envelope you, etc.) What did this memory feel like? (Include 1-3 Feeling Words.)

_____

Sketch a stick-figure-picture of this memory on the page to the left. (Include a stick sketch with the details you wrote above).

Ask, "Jesus, would you show me where you were in this memory?" If you sense his presence or see where he was, draw something to show where (cross, flame, etc.) OR draw where you sensed the most joy or peace. *Take a moment and thank Jesus for this memory and/or what you like about Jesus.

_____

_____

/   /20

Give thanks to the Lord, for he is good; his love endures forever.
1 Chronicles 16:34

I am thankful for...
1. _____
2. _____
3. _____

Jesus, what specific positive memory would be good for me to focus on in this moment? (30-60 seconds nothing comes to mind? Pick a memory & continue.)

_____

Some details in this memory are... (Include 1-2 Five Sense words.)

_____

_____

Take a moment. Allow yourself to experience the memory. Close your eyes. Picture being present in this specific memory. (Smell the trees, feel the liquid ocean envelope you, etc.) What did this memory feel like? (Include 1-3 Feeling Words.)

_____

Sketch a stick-figure-picture of this memory on the page to the left. (Include a stick sketch with the details you wrote above).

*Ask, "Jesus, would you show me where you were in this memory?" If you sense his presence or see where he was, draw something to show where (cross, flame, etc.) OR draw where you sensed the most joy or peace. *Take a moment and thank Jesus for this memory and/or what you like about Jesus.*

_____

_____

/   /20

The Lord your God is with you, the Mighty Warrior who saves. He will take great delight in you; in his love he will no longer rebuke you, but will rejoice over you with singing." Zephaniah 3:17

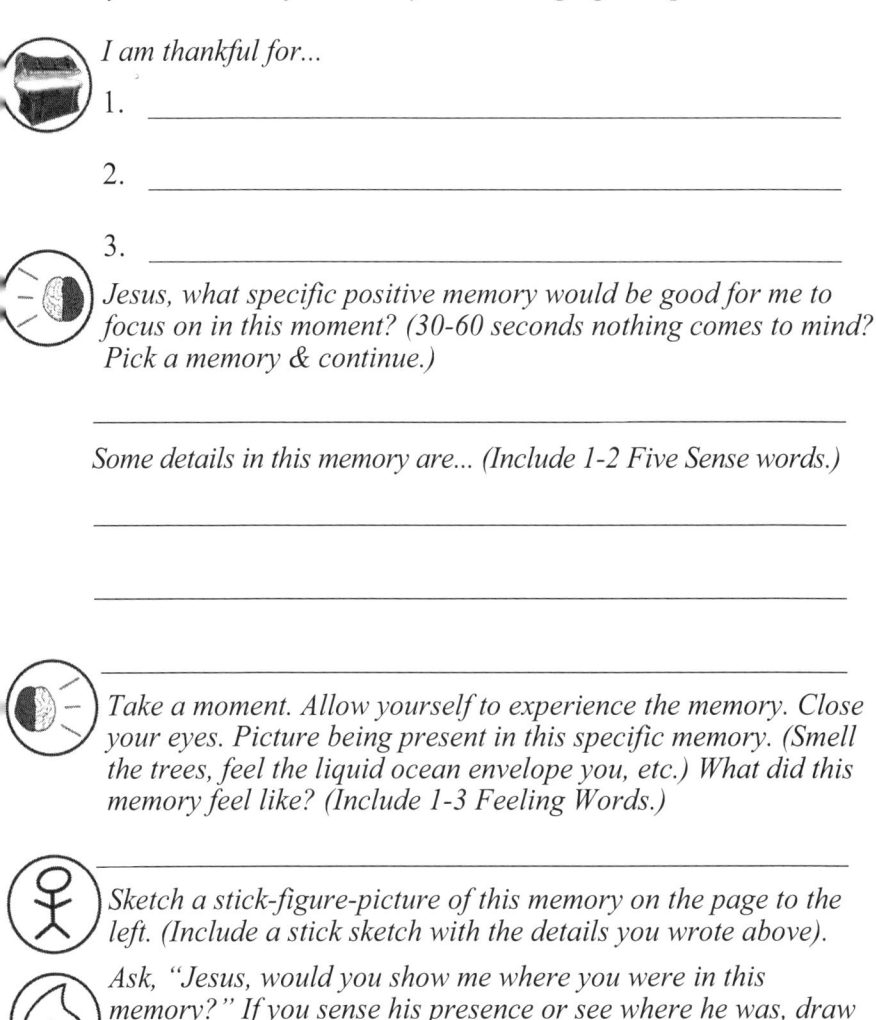

I am thankful for...
1. _____
2. _____
3. _____

Jesus, what specific positive memory would be good for me to focus on in this moment? (30-60 seconds nothing comes to mind? Pick a memory & continue.)

_____

Some details in this memory are... (Include 1-2 Five Sense words.)

_____
_____
_____

Take a moment. Allow yourself to experience the memory. Close your eyes. Picture being present in this specific memory. (Smell the trees, feel the liquid ocean envelope you, etc.) What did this memory feel like? (Include 1-3 Feeling Words.)

_____

Sketch a stick-figure-picture of this memory on the page to the left. (Include a stick sketch with the details you wrote above).

Ask, "Jesus, would you show me where you were in this memory?" If you sense his presence or see where he was, draw something to show where (cross, flame, etc.) OR draw where you sensed the most joy or peace. *Take a moment and thank Jesus for this memory and/or what you like about Jesus.

_____
_____

/   /20

Then he took a cup when he had given thanks, he gave it to them, saying, "Drink from it, all of you." Matthew 26:27

I am thankful for...
1. _____
2. _____
3. _____

Jesus, what specific positive memory would be good for me to focus on in this moment? (30-60 seconds nothing comes to mind? Pick a memory & continue.)

_____

Some details in this memory are... (Include 1-2 Five Sense words.)

_____

_____

_____

Take a moment. Allow yourself to experience the memory. Close your eyes. Picture being present in this specific memory. (Smell the trees, feel the liquid ocean envelope you, etc.) What did this memory feel like? (Include 1-3 Feeling Words.)

_____

Sketch a stick-figure-picture of this memory on the page to the left. (Include a stick sketch with the details you wrote above).

Ask, "Jesus, would you show me where you were in this memory?" If you sense his presence or see where he was, draw something to show where (cross, flame, etc.) OR draw where you sensed the most joy or peace. *Take a moment and thank Jesus for this memory and/or what you like about Jesus.

_____

_____

/   /20

But thanks be to God, who always leads us as captives in Christ's triumphal procession and uses us to spread the aroma of the knowledge of him everywhere. 2 Corinthians 2:14

I am thankful for...

1. _____

2. _____

3. _____

Jesus, what specific positive memory would be good for me to focus on in this moment? (30-60 seconds nothing comes to mind? Pick a memory & continue.)

_____

Some details in this memory are... (Include 1-2 Five Sense words.)

_____

_____

_____

Take a moment. Allow yourself to experience the memory. Close your eyes. Picture being present in this specific memory. (Smell the trees, feel the liquid ocean envelope you, etc.) What did this memory feel like? (Include 1-3 Feeling Words.)

_____

Sketch a stick-figure-picture of this memory on the page to the left. (Include a stick sketch with the details you wrote above).

Ask, "Jesus, would you show me where you were in this memory?" If you sense his presence or see where he was, draw something to show where (cross, flame, etc.) OR draw where you sensed the most joy or peace. *Take a moment and thank Jesus for this memory and/or what you like about Jesus.

_____

_____

/   /20

You will be enriched in every way so that you can be generous on every occasion, and through us your generosity will result in thanksgiving to God. 2 Corinthians 9:11

I am thankful for...
1. _____

2. _____

3. _____

Jesus, what specific positive memory would be good for me to focus on in this moment? (30-60 seconds nothing comes to mind? Pick a memory & continue.)

_____

Some details in this memory are... (Include 1-2 Five Sense words.)

_____

_____

_____

Take a moment. Allow yourself to experience the memory. Close your eyes. Picture being present in this specific memory. (Smell the trees, feel the liquid ocean envelope you, etc.) What did this memory feel like? (Include 1-3 Feeling Words.)

Sketch a stick-figure-picture of this memory on the page to the left. (Include a stick sketch with the details you wrote above).

Ask, "Jesus, would you show me where you were in this memory?" If you sense his presence or see where he was, draw something to show where (cross, flame, etc.) OR draw where you sensed the most joy or peace. *Take a moment and thank Jesus for this memory and/or what you like about Jesus.

_____

_____

/   /20

All this is for your benefit, so that the grace that is reaching more and more people may cause thanksgiving to overflow to the glory of God. 2 Corinthians 4:15

I am thankful for...

1. _____

2. _____

3. _____

Jesus, what specific positive memory would be good for me to focus on in this moment? (30-60 seconds nothing comes to mind? Pick a memory & continue.)

_____

Some details in this memory are... (Include 1-2 Five Sense words.)

_____

_____

_____

Take a moment. Allow yourself to experience the memory. Close your eyes. Picture being present in this specific memory. (Smell the trees, feel the liquid ocean envelope you, etc.) What did this memory feel like? (Include 1-3 Feeling Words.)

_____

Sketch a stick-figure-picture of this memory on the page to the left. (Include a stick sketch with the details you wrote above).

Ask, "Jesus, would you show me where you were in this memory?" If you sense his presence or see where he was, draw something to show where (cross, flame, etc.) OR draw where you sensed the most joy or peace. *Take a moment and thank Jesus for this memory and/or what you like about Jesus.

_____

_____

/   /20

I thank and praise you, God of my ancestors: You have given me wisdom and power, you have made known to me what we asked of you, you have made known to us the dream of the king. Daniel 2:23

I am thankful for...

1. _____

2. _____

3. _____

Jesus, what specific positive memory would be good for me to focus on in this moment? (30-60 seconds nothing comes to mind? Pick a memory & continue.)

_____

Some details in this memory are... (Include 1-2 Five Sense words.)

_____

_____

_____

Take a moment. Allow yourself to experience the memory. Close your eyes. Picture being present in this specific memory. (Smell the trees, feel the liquid ocean envelope you, etc.) What did this memory feel like? (Include 1-3 Feeling Words.)

_____

Sketch a stick-figure-picture of this memory on the page to the left. (Include a stick sketch with the details you wrote above).

*Ask, "Jesus, would you show me where you were in this memory?" If you sense his presence or see where he was, draw something to show where (cross, flame, etc.) OR draw where you sensed the most joy or peace. *Take a moment and thank Jesus for this memory and/or what you like about Jesus.*

_____

_____

/   /20

Cry out, "Save us, God our Savior; gather us and deliver us from the nations, that we may give thanks to your holy name, and glory in your praise." 1 Chronicles 16:35

I am thankful for...

1. _____

2. _____

3. _____

Jesus, what specific positive memory would be good for me to focus on in this moment? (30-60 seconds nothing comes to mind? Pick a memory & continue.)

_____

Some details in this memory are... (Include 1-2 Five Sense words.)

_____

_____

_____

Take a moment. Allow yourself to experience the memory. Close your eyes. Picture being present in this specific memory. (Smell the trees, feel the liquid ocean envelope you, etc.) What did this memory feel like? (Include 1-3 Feeling Words.)

Sketch a stick-figure-picture of this memory on the page to the left. (Include a stick sketch with the details you wrote above).

Ask, "Jesus, would you show me where you were in this memory?" If you sense his presence or see where he was, draw something to show where (cross, flame, etc.) OR draw where you sensed the most joy or peace. *Take a moment and thank Jesus for this memory and/or what you like about Jesus.

_____

_____

/   /20

I will give thanks to the Lord because of his righteousness; I will sing the praises of the name of the Lord Most High. Psalm 7:17

I am thankful for...
1. _____
2. _____
3. _____

Jesus, what specific positive memory would be good for me to focus on in this moment? (30-60 seconds nothing comes to mind? Pick a memory & continue.)

_____

Some details in this memory are... (Include 1-2 Five Sense words.)

_____
_____
_____

Take a moment. Allow yourself to experience the memory. Close your eyes. Picture being present in this specific memory. (Smell the trees, feel the liquid ocean envelope you, etc.) What did this memory feel like? (Include 1-3 Feeling Words.)

Sketch a stick-figure-picture of this memory on the page to the left. (Include a stick sketch with the details you wrote above).

Ask, "Jesus, would you show me where you were in this memory?" If you sense his presence or see where he was, draw something to show where (cross, flame, etc.) OR draw where you sensed the most joy or peace. *Take a moment and thank Jesus for this memory and/or what you like about Jesus.

_____
_____

/   /20

I will give you thanks in the great assembly; among the throngs I will praise you. Psalm 35:18

I am thankful for...
1. _____

2. _____

3. _____

Jesus, what specific positive memory would be good for me to focus on in this moment? (30-60 seconds nothing comes to mind? Pick a memory & continue.)

_____

Some details in this memory are... (Include 1-2 Five Sense words.)

_____

_____

_____

Take a moment. Allow yourself to experience the memory. Close your eyes. Picture being present in this specific memory. (Smell the trees, feel the liquid ocean envelope you, etc.) What did this memory feel like? (Include 1-3 Feeling Words.)

Sketch a stick-figure-picture of this memory on the page to the left. (Include a stick sketch with the details you wrote above).

Ask, "Jesus, would you show me where you were in this memory?" If you sense his presence or see where he was, draw something to show where (cross, flame, etc.) OR draw where you sensed the most joy or peace. *Take a moment and thank Jesus for this memory and/or what you like about Jesus.

_____

_____

/   /20

After he said this, he took some bread and gave thanks to God in front of them all. Then he broke it and began to eat. Acts 27:35

I am thankful for...
1. _____
2. _____
3. _____

Jesus, what specific positive memory would be good for me to focus on in this moment? (30-60 seconds nothing comes to mind? Pick a memory & continue.)

_____

Some details in this memory are... (Include 1-2 Five Sense words.)

_____

_____

_____

Take a moment. Allow yourself to experience the memory. Close your eyes. Picture being present in this specific memory. (Smell the trees, feel the liquid ocean envelope you, etc.) What did this memory feel like? (Include 1-3 Feeling Words.)

Sketch a stick-figure-picture of this memory on the page to the left. (Include a stick sketch with the details you wrote above).

Ask, "Jesus, would you show me where you were in this memory?" If you sense his presence or see where he was, draw something to show where (cross, flame, etc.) OR draw where you sensed the most joy or peace. *Take a moment and thank Jesus for this memory and/or what you like about Jesus.

_____

_____

/   /20

But thanks be to God! He gives us the victory through our Lord Jesus Christ. 1 Corinthians 15:57

I am thankful for...
1. _____

2. _____

3. _____

Jesus, what specific positive memory would be good for me to focus on in this moment? (30-60 seconds nothing comes to mind? Pick a memory & continue.)

_____

Some details in this memory are... (Include 1-2 Five Sense words.)

_____

_____

_____

Take a moment. Allow yourself to experience the memory. Close your eyes. Picture being present in this specific memory. (Smell the trees, feel the liquid ocean envelope you, etc.) What did this memory feel like? (Include 1-3 Feeling Words.)

Sketch a stick-figure-picture of this memory on the page to the left. (Include a stick sketch with the details you wrote above).

*Ask, "Jesus, would you show me where you were in this memory?" If you sense his presence or see where he was, draw something to show where (cross, flame, etc.) OR draw where you sensed the most joy or peace. *Take a moment and thank Jesus for this memory and/or what you like about Jesus.*

_____

_____

/   /20

Devote yourselves to prayer, being watchful and thankful.
Colossians 4:2

I am thankful for...
1. _____

2. _____

3. _____

Jesus, what specific positive memory would be good for me to focus on in this moment? (30-60 seconds nothing comes to mind? Pick a memory & continue.)

_____

Some details in this memory are... (Include 1-2 Five Sense words.)

_____

_____

_____

Take a moment. Allow yourself to experience the memory. Close your eyes. Picture being present in this specific memory. (Smell the trees, feel the liquid ocean envelope you, etc.) What did this memory feel like? (Include 1-3 Feeling Words.)

_____

Sketch a stick-figure-picture of this memory on the page to the left. (Include a stick sketch with the details you wrote above).

Ask, "Jesus, would you show me where you were in this memory?" If you sense his presence or see where he was, draw something to show where (cross, flame, etc.) OR draw where you sensed the most joy or peace. *Take a moment and thank Jesus for this memory and/or what you like about Jesus.

_____

_____

/   /20

Therefore, since we are receiving a kingdom that cannot be shaken, let us be thankful, and so worship God acceptably with reverence and awe, for our "God is a consuming fire. Hebrews 12:28-29

I am thankful for...
1. _____
2. _____
3. _____

Jesus, what specific positive memory would be good for me to focus on in this moment? (30-60 seconds nothing comes to mind? Pick a memory & continue.)

_____

Some details in this memory are... (Include 1-2 Five Sense words.)

_____
_____
_____

Take a moment. Allow yourself to experience the memory. Close your eyes. Picture being present in this specific memory. (Smell the trees, feel the liquid ocean envelope you, etc.) What did this memory feel like? (Include 1-3 Feeling Words.)

_____

Sketch a stick-figure-picture of this memory on the page to the left. (Include a stick sketch with the details you wrote above).

*Ask, "Jesus, would you show me where you were in this memory?" If you sense his presence or see where he was, draw something to show where (cross, flame, etc.) OR draw where you sensed the most joy or peace. *Take a moment and thank Jesus for this memory and/or what you like about Jesus.*

_____
_____

/   /20

Give thanks to God, our King over all gods! His tender love for us continues on forever! Psalm 136:2 TPT

I am thankful for...
1. _____
2. _____
3. _____

Jesus, what specific positive memory would be good for me to focus on in this moment? (30-60 seconds nothing comes to mind? Pick a memory & continue.)

_____

Some details in this memory are... (Include 1-2 Five Sense words.)

_____

_____

_____

Take a moment. Allow yourself to experience the memory. Close your eyes. Picture being present in this specific memory. (Smell the trees, feel the liquid ocean envelope you, etc.) What did this memory feel like? (Include 1-3 Feeling Words.)

_____

Sketch a stick-figure-picture of this memory on the page to the left. (Include a stick sketch with the details you wrote above).

*Ask, "Jesus, would you show me where you were in this memory?" If you sense his presence or see where he was, draw something to show where (cross, flame, etc.) OR draw where you sensed the most joy or peace. *Take a moment and thank Jesus for this memory and/or what you like about Jesus.*

_____

_____

/   /20

I will sing the Lord's praise, for he has been good to me. Psalm 13:6

I am thankful for...
1. _____
2. _____
3. _____

Jesus, what specific positive memory would be good for me to focus on in this moment? (30-60 seconds nothing comes to mind? Pick a memory & continue.)

_____

Some details in this memory are... (Include 1-2 Five Sense words.)

_____
_____

_____

Take a moment. Allow yourself to experience the memory. Close your eyes. Picture being present in this specific memory. (Smell the trees, feel the liquid ocean envelope you, etc.) What did this memory feel like? (Include 1-3 Feeling Words.)

_____

Sketch a stick-figure-picture of this memory on the page to the left. (Include a stick sketch with the details you wrote above).

*Ask, "Jesus, would you show me where you were in this memory?" If you sense his presence or see where he was, draw something to show where (cross, flame, etc.) OR draw where you sensed the most joy or peace. *Take a moment and thank Jesus for this memory and/or what you like about Jesus.*

_____
_____

/   /20

I will give you hidden treasures, riches stored in secret places, so that you may know that I am the Lord, the God of Israel, who summons you by name. Isaiah 45:3

I am thankful for...

1. _____

2. _____

3. _____

Jesus, what specific positive memory would be good for me to focus on in this moment? (30-60 seconds nothing comes to mind? Pick a memory & continue.)

_____

Some details in this memory are... (Include 1-2 Five Sense words.)

_____

_____

_____

Take a moment. Allow yourself to experience the memory. Close your eyes. Picture being present in this specific memory. (Smell the trees, feel the liquid ocean envelope you, etc.) What did this memory feel like? (Include 1-3 Feeling Words.)

Sketch a stick-figure-picture of this memory on the page to the left. (Include a stick sketch with the details you wrote above).

Ask, "Jesus, would you show me where you were in this memory?" If you sense his presence or see where he was, draw something to show where (cross, flame, etc.) OR draw where you sensed the most joy or peace. *Take a moment and thank Jesus for this memory and/or what you like about Jesus.

_____

_____

/   /20

Everyone come meet his face with a thankful heart. Don't hold back your praises; make him great by your shouts of joy!
Psalm 95:2 TPT

I am thankful for...

1. _____

2. _____

3. _____

Jesus, what specific positive memory would be good for me to focus on in this moment? (30-60 seconds nothing comes to mind? Pick a memory & continue.)

_____

Some details in this memory are... (Include 1-2 Five Sense words.)

_____

_____

_____

Take a moment. Allow yourself to experience the memory. Close your eyes. Picture being present in this specific memory. (Smell the trees, feel the liquid ocean envelope you, etc.) What did this memory feel like? (Include 1-3 Feeling Words.)

Sketch a stick-figure-picture of this memory on the page to the left. (Include a stick sketch with the details you wrote above).

Ask, "Jesus, would you show me where you were in this memory?" If you sense his presence or see where he was, draw something to show where (cross, flame, etc.) OR draw where you sensed the most joy or peace. *Take a moment and thank Jesus for this memory and/or what you like about Jesus.

_____

_____

/   /20

All the earth bows down to you; they sing praise to you, they sing the praises of your name. Psalm 66:4

I am thankful for...
1. _____

2. _____

3. _____

Jesus, what specific positive memory would be good for me to focus on in this moment? (30-60 seconds nothing comes to mind? Pick a memory & continue.)

_____

Some details in this memory are... (Include 1-2 Five Sense words.)

_____

_____

_____

Take a moment. Allow yourself to experience the memory. Close your eyes. Picture being present in this specific memory. (Smell the trees, feel the liquid ocean envelope you, etc.) What did this memory feel like? (Include 1-3 Feeling Words.)

Sketch a stick-figure-picture of this memory on the page to the left. (Include a stick sketch with the details you wrote above).

Ask, "Jesus, would you show me where you were in this memory?" If you sense his presence or see where he was, draw something to show where (cross, flame, etc.) OR draw where you sensed the most joy or peace. *Take a moment and thank Jesus for this memory and/or what you like about Jesus.

_____

_____

/   /20

I know what it is to be in need, and I know what it is to have plenty. I have learned the secret of being content in any and every situation, whether well fed or hungry, whether living in plenty or in want. Philippians 4:12

I am thankful for...

1. _____

2. _____

3. _____

Jesus, what specific positive memory would be good for me to focus on in this moment? (30-60 seconds nothing comes to mind? Pick a memory & continue.)

_____

Some details in this memory are... (Include 1-2 Five Sense words.)

_____

_____

_____

Take a moment. Allow yourself to experience the memory. Close your eyes. Picture being present in this specific memory. (Smell the trees, feel the liquid ocean envelope you, etc.) What did this memory feel like? (Include 1-3 Feeling Words.)

Sketch a stick-figure-picture of this memory on the page to the left. (Include a stick sketch with the details you wrote above).

Ask, "Jesus, would you show me where you were in this memory?" If you sense his presence or see where he was, draw something to show where (cross, flame, etc.) OR draw where you sensed the most joy or peace. *Take a moment and thank Jesus for this memory and/or what you like about Jesus.

_____

_____

/   /20

After the earthquake came a fire, but the Lord was not in the fire. And after the fire came a gentle whisper. 1 Kings 19:12

I am thankful for...

1. _____

2. _____

3. _____

Jesus, what specific positive memory would be good for me to focus on in this moment? (30-60 seconds nothing comes to mind? Pick a memory & continue.)

_____

Some details in this memory are... (Include 1-2 Five Sense words.)

_____

_____

_____

Take a moment. Allow yourself to experience the memory. Close your eyes. Picture being present in this specific memory. (Smell the trees, feel the liquid ocean envelope you, etc.) What did this memory feel like? (Include 1-3 Feeling Words.)

_____

Sketch a stick-figure-picture of this memory on the page to the left. (Include a stick sketch with the details you wrote above).

*Ask, "Jesus, would you show me where you were in this memory?" If you sense his presence or see where he was, draw something to show where (cross, flame, etc.) OR draw where you sensed the most joy or peace. *Take a moment and thank Jesus for this memory and/or what you like about Jesus.*

_____

_____

/   /20

With praise and thanksgiving they sang to the Lord: "He is good; his love toward Israel endures forever." And all the people gave a great shout of praise to the Lord, because the foundation of the house of the Lord was laid. Ezra 3:11

I am thankful for...
1. _____

2. _____

3. _____

Jesus, what specific positive memory would be good for me to focus on in this moment? (30-60 seconds nothing comes to mind? Pick a memory & continue.)

_____

Some details in this memory are... (Include 1-2 Five Sense words.)

_____

_____

Take a moment. Allow yourself to experience the memory. Close your eyes. Picture being present in this specific memory. (Smell the trees, feel the liquid ocean envelope you, etc.) What did this memory feel like? (Include 1-3 Feeling Words.)

_____

Sketch a stick-figure-picture of this memory on the page to the left. (Include a stick sketch with the details you wrote above).

Ask, "Jesus, would you show me where you were in this memory?" If you sense his presence or see where he was, draw something to show where (cross, flame, etc.) OR draw where you sensed the most joy or peace. *Take a moment and thank Jesus for this memory and/or what you like about Jesus.

_____

_____

/   /20

And behold, the glory of the God of Israel came from the way of the east. His voice was like the sound of many waters; and the earth shone with His glory. Ezekiel 43:2 NKJV

I am thankful for...

1. _____

2. _____

3. _____

Jesus, what specific positive memory would be good for me to focus on in this moment? (30-60 seconds nothing comes to mind? Pick a memory & continue.)

_____

Some details in this memory are... (Include 1-2 Five Sense words.)

_____

_____

_____

Take a moment. Allow yourself to experience the memory. Close your eyes. Picture being present in this specific memory. (Smell the trees, feel the liquid ocean envelope you, etc.) What did this memory feel like? (Include 1-3 Feeling Words.)

_____

Sketch a stick-figure-picture of this memory on the page to the left. (Include a stick sketch with the details you wrote above).

Ask, "Jesus, would you show me where you were in this memory?" If you sense his presence or see where he was, draw something to show where (cross, flame, etc.) OR draw where you sensed the most joy or peace. *Take a moment and thank Jesus for this memory and/or what you like about Jesus.

_____

_____

/   /20

Give thanks to the Lord, for he is good; his love endures forever.
Psalm 107:1

I am thankful for...
1. _____

2. _____

3. _____

Jesus, what specific positive memory would be good for me to focus on in this moment? (30-60 seconds nothing comes to mind? Pick a memory & continue.)

_____

Some details in this memory are... (Include 1-2 Five Sense words.)

_____

_____

_____

Take a moment. Allow yourself to experience the memory. Close your eyes. Picture being present in this specific memory. (Smell the trees, feel the liquid ocean envelope you, etc.) What did this memory feel like? (Include 1-3 Feeling Words.)

_____

Sketch a stick-figure-picture of this memory on the page to the left. (Include a stick sketch with the details you wrote above).

*Ask, "Jesus, would you show me where you were in this memory?" If you sense his presence or see where he was, draw something to show where (cross, flame, etc.) OR draw where you sensed the most joy or peace. *Take a moment and thank Jesus for this memory and/or what you like about Jesus.*

_____

_____

While they were eating, Jesus took bread, and when he had given thanks, he broke it and gave it to his disciples, saying, "Take and eat; this is my body." Matthew 26:26

I am thankful for...

1. _____

2. _____

3. _____

Jesus, what specific positive memory would be good for me to focus on in this moment? (30-60 seconds nothing comes to mind? Pick a memory & continue.)

_____

Some details in this memory are... (Include 1-2 Five Sense words.)

_____

_____

_____

Take a moment. Allow yourself to experience the memory. Close your eyes. Picture being present in this specific memory. (Smell the trees, feel the liquid ocean envelope you, etc.) What did this memory feel like? (Include 1-3 Feeling Words.)

_____

Sketch a stick-figure-picture of this memory on the page to the left. (Include a stick sketch with the details you wrote above).

Ask, "Jesus, would you show me where you were in this memory?" If you sense his presence or see where he was, draw something to show where (cross, flame, etc.) OR draw where you sensed the most joy or peace. *Take a moment and thank Jesus for this memory and/or what you like about Jesus.

_____

_____

/   /20

I always thank my God for you because of his grace given you in Christ Jesus. 1 Corinthians 1:4

I am thankful for...
1. _____
2. _____
3. _____

Jesus, what specific positive memory would be good for me to focus on in this moment? (30-60 seconds nothing comes to mind? Pick a memory & continue.)

_____

Some details in this memory are... (Include 1-2 Five Sense words.)

_____

_____

Take a moment. Allow yourself to experience the memory. Close your eyes. Picture being present in this specific memory. (Smell the trees, feel the liquid ocean envelope you, etc.) What did this memory feel like? (Include 1-3 Feeling Words.)

_____

Sketch a stick-figure-picture of this memory on the page to the left. (Include a stick sketch with the details you wrote above).

*Ask, "Jesus, would you show me where you were in this memory?" If you sense his presence or see where he was, draw something to show where (cross, flame, etc.) OR draw where you sensed the most joy or peace. *Take a moment and thank Jesus for this memory and/or what you like about Jesus.*

_____

_____

/ /20

And whatever you do, whether in word or deed, do it all in the name of the Lord Jesus, giving thanks to God the Father through him.
Colossians 3:17

I am thankful for...

1. _____

2. _____

3. _____

Jesus, what specific positive memory would be good for me to focus on in this moment? (30-60 seconds nothing comes to mind? Pick a memory & continue.)

_____

Some details in this memory are... (Include 1-2 Five Sense words.)

_____

_____

_____

Take a moment. Allow yourself to experience the memory. Close your eyes. Picture being present in this specific memory. (Smell the trees, feel the liquid ocean envelope you, etc.) What did this memory feel like? (Include 1-3 Feeling Words.)

Sketch a stick-figure-picture of this memory on the page to the left. (Include a stick sketch with the details you wrote above).

*Ask, "Jesus, would you show me where you were in this memory?" If you sense his presence or see where he was, draw something to show where (cross, flame, etc.) OR draw where you sensed the most joy or peace. *Take a moment and thank Jesus for this memory and/or what you like about Jesus.*

_____

_____

/   /20

My sheep listen to my voice; I know them, and they follow me. I give them eternal life, and they shall never perish; no one will snatch them out of my hand. John 10:27-28

I am thankful for...

1. _____

2. _____

3. _____

Jesus, what specific positive memory would be good for me to focus on in this moment? (30-60 seconds nothing comes to mind? Pick a memory & continue.)

_____

Some details in this memory are... (Include 1-2 Five Sense words.)

_____

_____

_____

Take a moment. Allow yourself to experience the memory. Close your eyes. Picture being present in this specific memory. (Smell the trees, feel the liquid ocean envelope you, etc.) What did this memory feel like? (Include 1-3 Feeling Words.)

Sketch a stick-figure-picture of this memory on the page to the left. (Include a stick sketch with the details you wrote above).

Ask, "Jesus, would you show me where you were in this memory?" If you sense his presence or see where he was, draw something to show where (cross, flame, etc.) OR draw where you sensed the most joy or peace. *Take a moment and thank Jesus for this memory and/or what you like about Jesus.

_____

_____

/   /20

This is the day the Lord has made;
We will rejoice and be glad in it. Psalm 118:24

I am thankful for...
1. _____

2. _____

3. _____

Jesus, what specific positive memory would be good for me to focus on in this moment? (30-60 seconds nothing comes to mind? Pick a memory & continue.)

_____

Some details in this memory are... (Include 1-2 Five Sense words.)

_____

_____

_____

Take a moment. Allow yourself to experience the memory. Close your eyes. Picture being present in this specific memory. (Smell the trees, feel the liquid ocean envelope you, etc.) What did this memory feel like? (Include 1-3 Feeling Words.)

_____

Sketch a stick-figure-picture of this memory on the page to the left. (Include a stick sketch with the details you wrote above).

*Ask, "Jesus, would you show me where you were in this memory?" If you sense his presence or see where he was, draw something to show where (cross, flame, etc.) OR draw where you sensed the most joy or peace. *Take a moment and thank Jesus for this memory and/or what you like about Jesus.*

_____

_____

/   /20

Lord, you have always been our eternal home, our hiding place from generation to generation. Psalm 90:1 TPT

I am thankful for...
1. _____
2. _____
3. _____

Jesus, what specific positive memory would be good for me to focus on in this moment? (30-60 seconds nothing comes to mind? Pick a memory & continue.)

_____

Some details in this memory are... (Include 1-2 Five Sense words.)

_____

_____

_____

Take a moment. Allow yourself to experience the memory. Close your eyes. Picture being present in this specific memory. (Smell the trees, feel the liquid ocean envelope you, etc.) What did this memory feel like? (Include 1-3 Feeling Words.)

_____

Sketch a stick-figure-picture of this memory on the page to the left. (Include a stick sketch with the details you wrote above).

Ask, "Jesus, would you show me where you were in this memory?" If you sense his presence or see where he was, draw something to show where (cross, flame, etc.) OR draw where you sensed the most joy or peace. *Take a moment and thank Jesus for this memory and/or what you like about Jesus.

_____

_____

/   /20

Sing to the Lord with grateful praise; make music to our God on the harp. Psalm 147:7

I am thankful for...

1. _____

2. _____

3. _____

Jesus, what specific positive memory would be good for me to focus on in this moment? (30-60 seconds nothing comes to mind? Pick a memory & continue.)

_____

Some details in this memory are... (Include 1-2 Five Sense words.)

_____

_____

_____

Take a moment. Allow yourself to experience the memory. Close your eyes. Picture being present in this specific memory. (Smell the trees, feel the liquid ocean envelope you, etc.) What did this memory feel like? (Include 1-3 Feeling Words.)

Sketch a stick-figure-picture of this memory on the page to the left. (Include a stick sketch with the details you wrote above).

Ask, "Jesus, would you show me where you were in this memory?" If you sense his presence or see where he was, draw something to show where (cross, flame, etc.) OR draw where you sensed the most joy or peace. *Take a moment and thank Jesus for this memory and/or what you like about Jesus.

_____

_____

The Lord will surely comfort Zion and will look with compassion on all her ruins; he will make her deserts like Eden, her wastelands like the garden of the Lord. Joy and gladness will be found in her, thanksgiving and the sound of singing. Isaiah 51:3

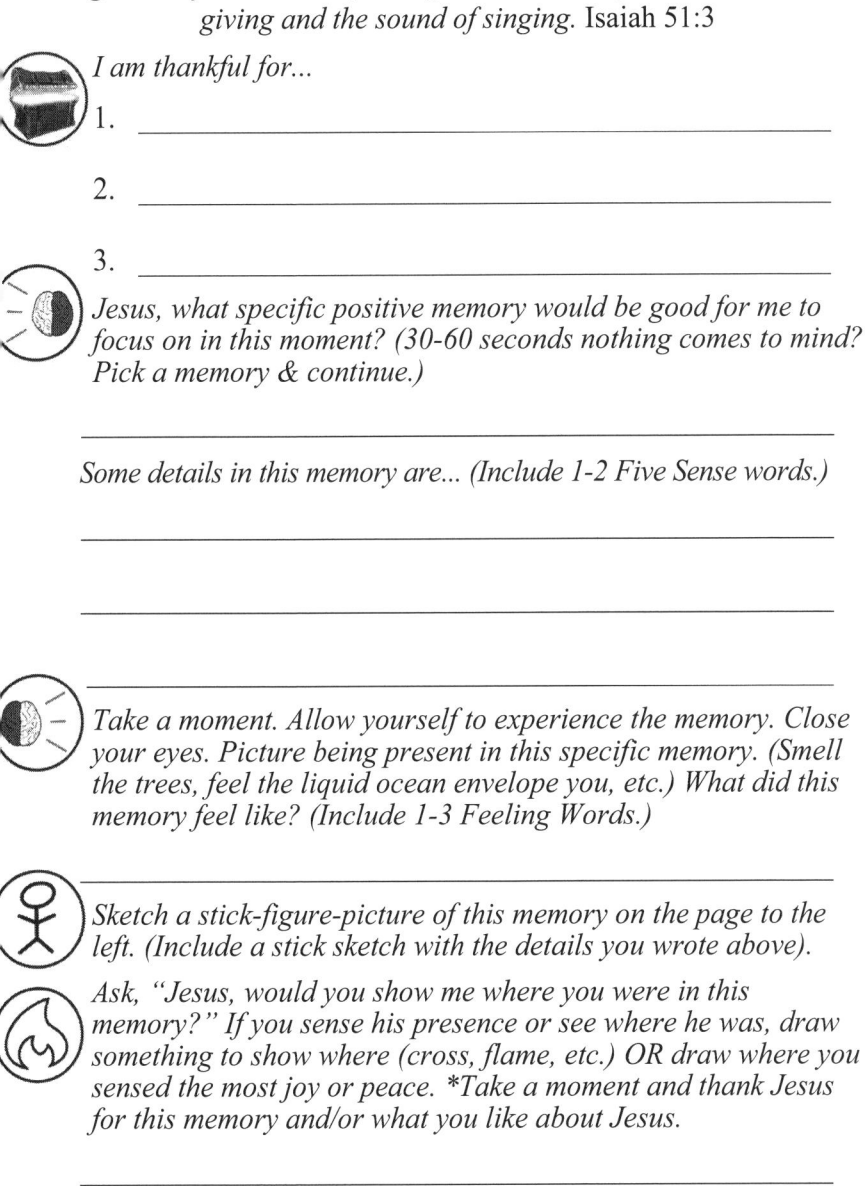

I am thankful for...

1. _____

2. _____

3. _____

Jesus, what specific positive memory would be good for me to focus on in this moment? (30-60 seconds nothing comes to mind? Pick a memory & continue.)

_____

Some details in this memory are... (Include 1-2 Five Sense words.)

_____

_____

Take a moment. Allow yourself to experience the memory. Close your eyes. Picture being present in this specific memory. (Smell the trees, feel the liquid ocean envelope you, etc.) What did this memory feel like? (Include 1-3 Feeling Words.)

_____

Sketch a stick-figure-picture of this memory on the page to the left. (Include a stick sketch with the details you wrote above).

Ask, "Jesus, would you show me where you were in this memory?" If you sense his presence or see where he was, draw something to show where (cross, flame, etc.) OR draw where you sensed the most joy or peace. *Take a moment and thank Jesus for this memory and/or what you like about Jesus.

_____

_____

/ /20

*Delight yourself in the Lord,
and he will give you the desires of your heart.*
Psalm 37:4 ESV

I am thankful for...

1. _____

2. _____

3. _____

Jesus, what specific positive memory would be good for me to focus on in this moment? (30-60 seconds nothing comes to mind? Pick a memory & continue.)

_____

Some details in this memory are... (Include 1-2 Five Sense words.)

_____

_____

_____

Take a moment. Allow yourself to experience the memory. Close your eyes. Picture being present in this specific memory. (Smell the trees, feel the liquid ocean envelope you, etc.) What did this memory feel like? (Include 1-3 Feeling Words.)

_____

Sketch a stick-figure-picture of this memory on the page to the left. (Include a stick sketch with the details you wrote above).

*Ask, "Jesus, would you show me where you were in this memory?" If you sense his presence or see where he was, draw something to show where (cross, flame, etc.) OR draw where you sensed the most joy or peace. *Take a moment and thank Jesus for this memory and/or what you like about Jesus.*

_____

_____

/   /20

Don't copy the behavior and customs of this world, but let God transform you into a new person by changing the way you think. Then you will learn to know God's will for you, which is good and pleasing and perfect. Romans 12:2 NLT

I am thankful for...

1. _____

2. _____

3. _____

Jesus, what specific positive memory would be good for me to focus on in this moment? (30-60 seconds nothing comes to mind? Pick a memory & continue.)

_____

Some details in this memory are... (Include 1-2 Five Sense words.)

_____

_____

Take a moment. Allow yourself to experience the memory. Close your eyes. Picture being present in this specific memory. (Smell the trees, feel the liquid ocean envelope you, etc.) What did this memory feel like? (Include 1-3 Feeling Words.)

_____

Sketch a stick-figure-picture of this memory on the page to the left. (Include a stick sketch with the details you wrote above).

Ask, "Jesus, would you show me where you were in this memory?" If you sense his presence or see where he was, draw something to show where (cross, flame, etc.) OR draw where you sensed the most joy or peace. *Take a moment and thank Jesus for this memory and/or what you like about Jesus.

_____

_____

Congratulations!

You completed 40 Jesus with me journal moments!!

Tools for practicing God's presence in everyday life.

Printed in Great Britain
by Amazon